pharmakon

Eugene Thacker

pharmakon

COSMIC PESSIMISM

Original Artwork by Keith Tilford

UNIVOCAL

Cosmic Pessimism
by Eugene Thacker

First Edition
Minneapolis © 2015, Univocal Publishing

Published by Univocal
123 North 3rd Street, #202
Minneapolis, MN 55401

Artwork: acrylic on duralar.
All images copyright Keith Tilford.

Designed & Printed by Jason Wagner
Distributed by the University of Minnesota Press

ISBN 9781937561475

Library of Congress Control Number 2015940595

~ * ~

There is no philosophy of pessimism,
only the reverse.

~ * ~

Cosmic Pessimism

Cosmic Pessimism

We're Doomed. Pessimism is the night-side of thought, a melodrama of the futility of the brain, a poetry written in the graveyard of philosophy. Pessimism is a lyrical failure of philosophical thinking, each attempt at clear and coherent thought, sullen and submerged in the hidden joy of its own futility. The closest pessimism comes to philosophical argument is the droll and laconic "We'll never make it," or simply: "We're doomed." Every effort doomed to failure, every project doomed to incompletion, every life doomed to be unlived, every thought doomed to be unthought.

Pessimism is the lowest form of philosophy, frequently disparaged and dismissed, merely the symptom of a bad attitude. No one ever needs pessimism, in the way that one needs optimism to inspire one to great heights and to pick oneself up, in the way one needs constructive criticism, advice and feedback, inspirational books or a pat on the back. No one needs pessimism (though I like to imagine the idea of pessimist self-help). No one needs pessimism, and yet everyone — without exception — has, at some point in their lives, had to confront pessimism, if not as a philosophy then as a grievance — against one's self or others, against one's surroundings or one's life, against the state of things or the world in general.

There is little redemption for pessimism, and no consolation prize. Ultimately, pessimism is weary of everything and of itself. Pessimism is the philosophical form of disenchantment — disenchantment as chanting, a chant, a mantra, a solitary, monophonic voice rendered insignificant by the intimate immensity surrounding it.

~ * ~

We're Still Doomed. No one has time for pessimism. After all, there are only so many hours in a day. Whatever our temperament, happy or sad, engaged or disengaged, we know pessimism when we hear it. The pessimist is usually understood as the complainer, forever pointing out what is wrong without ever once offering a solution. But more often than not pessimists are the *quietest* of philosophers,

4

submerging their own sighs within the lethargy of discontent. What little sound it makes is of interest to no one — "I've heard it all before," "tell me something I don't know," sound and fury, signifying nothing. In raising problems without solutions, in posing questions without answers, in retreating to the hermetic, cavernous abode of complaint, pessimism is guilty of that most inexcusable of Occidental crimes — the crime of not pretending it's for real. Pessimism fails to live up to the most basic tenet of philosophy — the "as if." Think as if it will be helpful, act as if it will make a difference, speak as if there is something to say, live as if you are not, in fact, being lived by some murmuring non-entity both shadowy and muddied.

Had it more self-assurance and better social skills, pessimism would turn its disenchantment into a religion, possibly calling itself The Great Refusal. But there is a negation in pessimism that refuses even such a Refusal, an awareness that, from the start, it has already failed, and that the culmination of all that is, is that all is for naught.

Pessimism tries very hard to present itself in the low, sustained tones of a Requiem Mass, or the tectonic rumbling of Tibetan chant. But it frequently lets loose dissonant notes at once plaintive and pathetic. Often, its voice cracks, its weighty words abruptly reduced to mere shards of guttural sound.

Maybe It's Not So Bad, After All. If we know pessimism when we hear it, this is because we've heard it all before — and we didn't need to hear it in the first place. Life is hard enough. What you need is a change of attitude, a new outlook, a shift in perspective ... a cup of coffee.

If we have no ears for pessimism, this is because it is always reducible to something as mutable as a voice. If pessimism is so frequently disparaged, it is because it brings everyone down, determined as it is to view each day as a bad day, if only by virtue of the fact that it is not yet a bad day. For pessimism the world is brimming with negative possibility, the collision of a bad mood with an impassive world. In fact, pessimism is the result of a confusion between the world and a statement about the world, a confusion that also prevents it from fully entering the hallowed halls of philosophy. If pessimism is so often dismissed, this is because it is often impossible to separate a "bad mood" from a philosophical proposition (and do not all philosophies stem from a bad mood?).

The very term "pessimism" suggests a school of thought, a movement, even a community. But pessimism always has a membership of one — maybe two. Ideally, of course, it would have a membership of none, with only a scribbled, illegible note left behind by someone long forgotten. But this seems unrealistic, though one can always hope.

~ * ~

Anatomy of Pessimism. Though it may locate itself at the margins of philosophy, pessimism is as much subject to philosophical analysis as any other form of thought.

Pessimism's lyricism of failure gives it the structure of music. What time is to the music of sorrow, reason is to a philosophy of the worst. Pessimism's two major keys are moral and metaphysical pessimism, its subjective and objective poles, an attitude towards the world and a claim about the world. For moral pessimism, it is better not to have been born at all; for metaphysical pessimism, this is the worst of all possible worlds. For moral pessimism the problem is the solipsism of human beings, the world made in our own image, a world-for-us. For metaphysical pessimism, the problem is the solipsism of the world, objected and projected as a world-in-itself. Both moral and metaphysical pessimism are compromised philosophically; moral pessimism by its failure to locate the human within a larger, non-human context, and metaphysical pessimism by its failure to recognize the complicity in the very claim of realism.

This is how pessimism makes its music of the worst, a generalized misanthropy without the *anthropos*. Pessimism crystallizes around this futility — it is its *amor fati*, rendered as musical form.

~ * ~

Melancholy of Anatomy. There is a logic of pessimism that is fundamental to its suspicion of philosophical system. Pessimism involves a *statement* about a *condition*. In pessimism each statement boils down to an affirmation or a negation, just as any condition boils down to the best or the worst.

With Schopenhauer, that arch-pessimist, the thinker for whom the philosopher and the curmudgeon perfectly overlap, we see a no-saying to the worst, a no-saying that secretly covets a yes-saying (through asceticism, mysticism, quietism), even if this hidden yes-saying is a horizon at the limits of comprehension. With Nietzsche comes the pronouncement of a Dionysian pessimism, a pessimism of strength or joy, a yes-saying to the worst, a yes-saying to this world as it is. And with Cioran yet another variation, unavailing yet lyrical, a no-saying to the worst, and a further no-saying to the possibility of any other world, in here or out there. With these one approaches, but never reaches, a studied abandonment of pessimism itself.

The logic of pessimism moves through three refusals: a no-saying to the worst (refusal of the world-for-us, or Schopenhauer's tears); a yes-saying to the worst (refusal of the world-in-itself, or Nietzsche's laughter); and a no-saying to the for-us and the in-itself (a double refusal, or Cioran's sleep).

Crying, laughing, sleeping — what other responses are adequate to a life that is so indifferent?

~ * ~

Cosmic Pessimism. Both moral and metaphysical pessimism point to another kind, a pessimism that is neither subjective nor objective, neither for-us nor in-itself, and instead a pessimism of the world-without-us. We could call this a *cosmic pessimism* ... but this sounds too majestic, too full of wonder, too much the bitter aftertaste of the Great Beyond. Words falter. And so do ideas. And so we have a cosmic pessimism, a pessimism that is first and last a pessimism about *cosmos*, about the necessity and possibility of order. The contours of cosmic pessimism are a drastic scaling-up or scaling-down of the human point of view, the unhuman orientation of deep space and deep time, and all of this shadowed by an impasse, a primordial insignificance, the impossibility of ever adequately accounting for one's relationship to thought — all that remains of pessimism is the desiderata of affects — agonistic, impassive, defiant, reclusive, filled with sorrow and flailing at that architectonic chess match called philosophy, a flailing that pessimism tries to raise to the level of an art form (though what usually results is slapstick).

~ * ~

Pessimism always falls short of being philosophical. My back aches, my knees hurt, I couldn't sleep last night, I'm stressed out, and I think I'm finally coming down with something. Pessimism abjures all pretenses towards system — towards the purity of analysis and the dignity of critique. We didn't really think we could figure it out, did we? It was just passing time, something to do, a bold gesture put forth in all its fragility, according to rules that we have agreed to forget that we made up in the first place. Every thought marked by a shadowy incomprehension that precedes it, and a futility that undermines it. That pessimism speaks, in whatever voice, is the singing testimony to this futility and this incomprehension — take a chance and step outside, lose some sleep and say you tried....

~ * ~

Song of Futility. Futility pervades pessimism. Futility, however, is different from fatality, and different again from simple failure (though failure is never simple). Failure is a breakage within the heart of relations, a fissure between cause and effect, a fissure hastily covered over by trying and trying again. With failure, there is always plenty of blame to go around; it's not my fault, it's a technical difficulty, it's a miscommunication.

For the pessimist, failure is a question of "when," not "if" — failure as a metaphysical principle. Everything withers and passes into an obscurity blacker than night, everything from the melodramatic decline of a person's life to the banal flickering moments that constitute each day. Everything that is done undone, everything said or known destined for a stellar oblivion.

When scaled up in this way, failure becomes fatality. Fatality is the hermeticism of cause and effect. In fatality, everything you do, whatever you do, always leads to a certain end, and ultimately to *the* end — though that end, or the means to that end, remain shrouded in obscurity. Nothing you do makes a difference because everything you do makes a difference. Hence the effects of your actions are hidden from you, even as you deceive yourself into thinking that this time you will outwit the order of things. By having a goal, planning ahead, and thinking things through carefully, we attempt, in a daily Prometheanism, to turn fatality to our advantage, to gain a glimpse of an order that seems buried deeper and deeper in the fabric of the universe.

But even fatality has its comforts. The chain of cause and effect may be hidden from us, but that's just because disorder is the order we don't yet see; it's just complex, distributed, and requires advanced mathematics. Fatality still clings to the sufficiency of everything that exists....When fatality relinquishes even this idea, it becomes futility. Futility arises out of the grim suspicion that, behind the shroud of causality we drape over the world, there is only the indifference of what exists or doesn't exist; whatever you do ultimately leads to no end, an irrevocable chasm between thought and world. Futility transforms the act of thinking into a zero-sum game.

~ * ~

Song of the Worst. At the center of pessimism lies the term *pessimus*, "the worst," a term as relative as it is absolute. The worst is about as bad as it gets, shrouded by the passage of time or the twists and turns of fortune. For the pessimist, "the worst" is the propensity for suffering that gradually occludes each living moment, until it is eclipsed entirely, overlapping perfectly in death ... which, for the pessimist, is no longer "the worst."

Pessimism is marked by an unwillingness to move beyond "the worst," something only partially attributable to a lack in motivation. In pessimism "the worst" is the ground that gives way beneath every existent — things could be worse, *and*, things could be better. "The worst" invariably implies a value judgment, one made based on scant evidence and little experience; in this way, pessimism's greatest nemesis is its moral orientation.

Perhaps this is why optimists are often the most severe pessimists — they are optimists that have run out of options. It seems that sooner or later we are all doomed to become optimists of this sort (the most depressing of thoughts...).

~ * ~

Song of Doom. Gloom and doom are the forms of consolation for any pessimist philosophy. Neither quite affects nor quite concepts, gloom and doom transform pessimism into a mortification of philosophy.

Doom is not just the sense that all things will turn out badly, but that all things inevitably come to an end, irrespective of whether or not they really do come to an end. What emerges from doom is a sense of the unhuman as an attractor, a horizon towards which the human is fatally drawn. Doom is humanity given over to unhumanity in an act of crystalline self-abnegation.

Gloom is not simply the anxiety that precedes doom. Gloom is atmospheric, climate as much as impression, and if people are also gloomy, this is simply the by-product of an anodyne atmosphere that only incidentally involves human beings. More climatological than psychological, gloom is the stuff of dim, hazy, overcast skies, of ruins and overgrown tombs, of a misty, lethargic fog that moves with the same languorousness as our own crouched and sullen listening to a disinterested world.

In a sense, gloom is the counterpoint to doom — what futility is to the former, fatality is to the latter. Doom is marked by temporality — all things precariously drawn to their end — whereas gloom is the austerity of stillness, all things sad, static, and suspended, hovering over cold lichen stones and damp fir trees. If doom is the terror of temporality and death, then gloom is the horror of a hovering stasis that is life.

I like to imagine that this realization alone is the thread that connects the charnel ground Aghori and the poets of the Graveyard School.

~ * ~

Song of Spite. There is an intolerance in pessimism that knows no bounds. In pessimism spite begins by fixing on a particular object of spite — someone one hardly knows, or someone one knows too well; a spite for this person or a spite for all of humanity; a spectacular or a banal spite; a spite for a noisy neighbor, a yapping dog, a battalion of strollers, the meandering idiot walking in front of you on their smart phone, large loud celebrations, traumatic injustices anywhere in the world regurgitated as media blitz, spite for the self-absorbed and overly performative people talking way too loud at the table next to you, technical difficulties and troubleshooting, the reduction of everything to branding, spite of the refusal to admit one's own errors, of self-help books, of people who know absolutely everything and make sure to tell you, of all people, all living beings, all things, the world, the spiteful planet, the inanity of existence....

Spite is the motor of pessimism because it is so egalitarian, so expansive, it runs amok, stumbling across intuitions that can only half-heartedly be called philosophical. Spite lacks the confidence and the clarity of hatred, but it also lacks the almost cordial judgment of dislike. For the pessimist, the smallest detail can be an indication of a metaphysical futility so vast and funereal that it eclipses pessimism itself — a spite that pessimism carefully places beyond the horizon of intelligibility, like the experience of dusk, or like the phrase "it is raining jewels and daggers."

~ * ~

Cioran once called music a "physics of tears." If this is true, then perhaps metaphysics is its commentary. Or its apology.

~ * ~

We do not live, we are lived. What would a philosophy have to be to begin from this, rather than to arrive at it?

~ * ~

Song of Sorrow. Nietzsche, commenting on pessimism, once castigated Schopenhauer for taking things too lightly. He writes: "Schopenhauer, though a pessimist, *really* — played the flute. Every day, after dinner: one should read his biography on that. And incidentally: a pessimist, one who denies God and the world but *comes to a stop* before morality — who affirms morality and plays the flute ... what? Is that really — a pessimist?"

We know that Schopenhauer did possess a collection of instruments, and we also know that Nietzsche himself composed music. There is no reason to think that either of them would ever banish music from the Republic of philosophy.

But Nietzsche's jibes at Schopenhauer are as much about music as they are about pessimism. For the pessimist who says no to everything and yet finds comfort in music, the no-saying of pessimism can only be a weak way of saying yes — the weightiest statement undercut by the flightiest of replies. The least that Schopenhauer could've done is to play the bass.

I'm not a big fan of the flute, or, for that matter, wind instruments generally. But what Nietzsche forgets is the role that the flute has historically played in Greek tragedy. In tragedy, the flute (*aulos*) is not an instrument of levity and joy, but of solitude and sorrow. The Greek *aulos* not only expresses the grief of tragic loss, but it does so in a way that renders weeping and singing inseparable from each other. Scholars of Greek tragedy refer to this as the "mourning voice." Set apart from the more official civic rituals of funerary mourning, the mourning voice of Greek tragedy constantly threatens to dissolve song into wailing, music into moaning, and the voice into a primordial, disarticulate anti-music. The mourning voice delineates all the forms of suffering — tears, weeping, sobbing, wailing, moaning, and the convulsions of thought reduced to an elemental unintelligibility.

Have we rescued Schopenhauer from Nietzsche? Probably not. Perhaps Schopenhauer played the flute to remind himself of the real function of the mourning voice — sorrow, sighs, and moaning rendered indistinguishable from music, the crumbling of the human into the unhuman. The highest failure of pessimism.

~ * ~

Song of Nothing. In Buddhist thought, the First Noble Truth is encapsulated in the Pali term *dukkha*, conventionally translated as "suffering," "sorrow," or "misery."

It is likely that Schopenhauer, reading the Buddhist texts available to him, recognized some filiation with the concept of *dukkha*. But this is a multi-faceted term. There is, certainly, *dukkha* in the usual sense of the suffering, strife, and loss associated with living a life. But this is, in turn, dependent on finitude and temporality, existence as determined by impermanence and imperfection. And this ultimately points to the way in which both suffering and finitude are grounded by the paradoxical ground-lessness of *dukkha* as a metaphysical principle — the insubstantiality and the emptiness of all that is. Beyond what is worse for me, beyond a world ordered for the worst, there is the emptiness of impersonal suffering ... the tears of the cosmos.

In this context, it is easy to see how Schopenhauer's pessimism attempts to compress all the aspects of *dukkha* into a nothingness at the core of existence, a "Willlessness" (*Willenlosigkeit*) coursing through the Will. Though one thing for certain is that with Schopenhauer we do not find the "ever-smiling" countenance of the Buddha — or do we?

The texts of the Pali Canon also contain lists of the different types of happiness — including the happiness of renunciation and the rather strange happiness of detachment. But Buddhism considers even the different types of happiness as part of *dukkha*, in this final sense of nothingness or emptiness. Perhaps Schopenhauer understood Buddhism better than he is usually given credit for. Empty sorrow, a lyricism of indifference. The result is a strange, and ultimately untenable, nocturnal form of Buddhism.

~ * ~

Song of Sleep. Somnus, known also by his Greek name Hypnos, is the god of sleep — and not the god of dreams. Somnus makes a brief appearance in Ovid's *Metamorphoses*, where he is depicted as living in a dark cave, cloaked in a kind of perpetual slumber. Like cats, Somnus is asleep more than he is awake, rendering the terms asleep and awake problematic.

In the 1920s, the Surrealist poet Robert Desnos is participating in the séances conducted at André Breton's apartment on rue de Fontaine. But when the Surrealists' "period of the sleeping fits" began, it was nothing more than a pretentious parlor game, poets playing with a Ouija board. That was until Desnos showed up. It turned out he was — much to his own surprise — quite gifted at putting himself to sleep. He could do it at a moment's notice, even in the middle of a bustling Parisian café. In this state, he could be questioned and would give strange and surprising replies, sometimes speaking and sometimes writing, sometimes even drawing. When prompted, he would divulge entire fantastical narratives, interweaving elements from myth and popular culture, overlaid with a lyricism still unparalleled in the literature of the period. One of Desnos' books from this period is titled *Mourning for Mourning*: "But what will human beings have to say when confronted by these great mobilizations of the mineral and vegetable worlds, being themselves the unstable plaything of the whirlwind's farcical games and of the marriage between the lesser elements and the chasms which separate the resounding words?"

~ * ~

Pessimism: the failure of sound and sense, the disarticulation of *phone* and *logos*.

~ * ~

You, the Night, and the Music. In a suggestive passage, Schopenhauer once noted that "music is the melody to which the world is the text."

Given Schopenhauer's view on life — that life is suffering, that human life is absurd, that the nothingness before my birth is equal to the nothingness after my death — given all this, one wonders what kind of music Schopenhauer had in mind when he described music as the melody to which the world is text — was it opera, a Requiem Mass, a madrigal, or perhaps a drinking song? Or something like *Eine kleine Nachtmusik*, a little night music for the twilight of thought, a sullen *nocturne* for the night-side of logic, an era of sad wings sung by a solitary banshee.

Perhaps the music Schopenhauer had in mind is music eliminated to non-music. A whisper would suffice. Perhaps a sigh of fatigue or resignation, perhaps a moan of despair or sorrow. Perhaps a sound just articulate enough that it could be heard to dissipate.

~ * ~

Everything dissipates into ether and weightless rains. In the submerged quiet kelp-like crystals wordlessly emerge. Seas of indifference.

~ * ~

The Tears of Kant. Cioran once wrote, "I turned away from philosophy when it became impossible to discover in Kant any human weakness, any authentic accent of melancholy, in Kant and in all the philosophers." I keep returning to Kant, but for the opposite reason. Each time I read, and witness the scintillating and austere construction of a system, I cannot help but to feel a certain sadness — the edifice itself is somehow depressing.

~ * ~

If a thinker like Schopenhauer has any redeeming qualities, it is that he identified the great lie of Western culture — the preference for existence over non-existence. As he notes: "If we knocked on the graves and asked the dead whether they would like to rise again, they would shake their heads."

In Western cultures it is commonly accepted that one celebrates birth and mourns death. But there must be a mistake here. Wouldn't it make more sense to mourn birth and celebrate death? Strange though, because the mourning of birth would, presumably, last the entirety of that person's life, so that mourning and living would be the same thing.

~ * ~

Human beings deep in thought look like corpses.

~ * ~

Paraphrase of Schopenhauer: what death is for the organism, sleep is for the individual. Resting, we wander far. Sleeping, we go nowhere.

~ * ~

The Patron Saints of Pessimism. There exist patron saints of philosophy, though their stories are not happy ones. There is, for instance, the fourth century Saint Catherine of Alexandria, or Catherine of the Wheel, named after the torture device used on her. A precocious fourteen year old scholar, Catherine was subject to continual persecution. After all forms of torture failed — including the "breaking wheel" — the emperor finally settled for her decapitation, a violent yet appropriate reminder of the protector of philosophers.

Does pessimism not deserve its own patron saints, even if they are unworthy of martyrdom? But in our search, even the most ardent nay-sayers frequently lapse into brief moments of enthusiasm — Pascal's love of solitude, Leopardi's love of poetry, Schopenhauer's love of music, Nietzsche's love of Schopenhauer, and so on. Should one then focus on individual works of pessimism? We could include Kierkegaard's trilogy of existential horror: *Sickness Unto Death*, *The Concept of Dread*, and *Fear and Trembling*, but all these are undermined by their fabricated and unreliable authors. Besides, how can one separate the pessimist from the optimist in works like Unamuno's *The Tragic Sense of Life* or Camus' *The Myth of Sisyphus*? And what of the many forgotten treatises on pessimism, of which Edgar Saltus' *The Philosophy of Disenchantment* is emblematic? Or the forgotten followers of Schopenhauer, some of them, like Philipp Mainländer, having committed suicide immediately after completing their books? And this is to say nothing of literary pessimism: Goethe's sorrowful Werther, Dostoevsky's underground creature, Pessoa's disquiet scribbler; Baudelaire's spleen and ennui, the mystical Satanism of Huysmans and Strindberg, the haunted and shimmering prose of Mário de Sá-Carniero, Izumi Kyōka, Clarice Lispector; the crumbling of reason from Artaud's *The Umbilicus of Limbo* to Unica Zürn's *House of Illnesses*. Grumpy old Beckett ... even the great pessimist stand-up comedians. All that remains is a litany of partial quotes and citations crammed into arborous fortune cookies.

Patron saints are traditionally named after a locale, either a place of birth or of a mystical experience. Perhaps the better approach is to focus on the places where pessimists were forced to live out their pessimism — Schopenhauer facing an empty Berlin lecture hall, Nietzsche mute and convalescent at the home of his sister, Wittgenstein the relinquished professor and solitary gardener, Cioran grappling with Alzheimer's in his tiny writing alcove in the Latin Quarter.

Laconic and sullen, the patron saints of pessimism never seem to do a good job at protecting, interceding, or advocating for those who suffer. Perhaps they need us more than we need them.

~ * ~

There's a ghost that grows inside of us, damaged in the making, and there's a hunt sprung from necessity, elliptical and drowned. Where the moving quiet of our insomnia offers up each thought, there's a luminous field of grey inertia, and obsidian dreams burnt all the way down.

~ * ~

Senilia. In the 1830s, fleeing a cholera epidemic in Berlin, Schopenhauer writes the following in his notebook:

> When I was seventeen, without any proper schooling, I was affected by the misery and wretchedness of life, as was the Buddha when in his youth he caught sight of sickness, old age, pain and death ... the result for me was that this world could not be the work of an all-bountiful, infinitely good being, but rather of a demon who had summoned into existence creatures in order to gloat over the sight of their anguish and agony.

Now, Schopenhauer was no Buddha, but the passage reveals something at the core of his thinking, and that is the dual origin of pessimism. On the one hand, pessimism is conditional, it stems from observation and experience, but also from inclination and predilection — maybe you're stressed out, maybe you're feeling down, maybe something somewhere hurts. This conditional pessimism can be found in Pascal, Lichtenberg, the French moralists, and it surfaces in Schopenhauer's many grumblings concerning humanity, caught as it is in the pedantic, existential metronome of boredom and striving.

But Schopenhauer also makes reference to another origin of pessimism that is unconditional, a kind of metaphysical suffering that is tantamount to existing itself, regardless of our attempts to tailor everything to the sufficient reasons that form the bedrock of philosophy — all forms of access are at best shadow plays that, in the end, mock the human form. But this metaphysical pessimism must itself fail — by definition.

If Schopenhauer's philosophy is pessimistic, it is because pessimism is caught somewhere between philosophy and a bad attitude, the syllogism entombed in the morose refusal of everything that is, a starless, luminous refusal of every principle of sufficiency — the futility of philosophy, in the key of philosophy. In one of his last notebooks — to which he gave the title "Senilia," Schopenhauer writes: "I can bear the thought that in a short time worms will eat away my body; but the idea of philosophy-professors nibbling at my philosophy makes me shudder."

~ * ~

Around you this night a thousand million firefly anatomies breathe in and out in their slow-burning liturgical glow.

~ * ~

The Abyss of a Book. Schopenhauer, using the metaphors of astronomy, once noted that there were three types of writers: meteors (the flare of fads and trends), planets (the faithful rotation of tradition), and the fixed stars (impervious and unwavering). But in Schopenhauer's own writing — aphorisms, fragments, stray thoughts — one is acutely aware of the way that all writing ultimately negates itself, either to be forgotten or to have been so precise that it results in silence.

Was Schopenhauer aware that he himself was a fourth type of writer — the black hole?

The Abyss of a Notebook. Nietzsche once lauded the value of the "incomplete thought" for philosophy. If we were to take this up, perhaps the best place to look for incomplete thoughts would be in the notebooks of philosophers. Nietzsche himself was a fastidious user of his notebooks, often writing on the right-hand side only and then flipping the notebook over, allowing him to fill notebooks front-to-back and back-to-front. This economy of the page was, perhaps, offset by Nietzsche's notoriously unreadable handwriting.

Schopenhauer, no less fastidious than Nietzsche, preferred to keep several notebooks going at once, notebooks of all sizes and types - octavo, quarto, folio, bound and unbound. Some notebooks remained fixed on his desk at home, while others could be taken with him on walks, and still other notebooks were reserved for traveling. And then there is Cioran, that gloomy prowler of the Latin Quarter, who was fond of the bright, multi-colored, spiral notebooks used by students....

It's almost as if the notebook mitigates against the book, if the former is not, in the end, negated by the latter. As Nietzsche notes, the incomplete thought "displays the most beautiful butterfly wings — and it slips away from us." I'm assuming that Nietzsche distinguishes the incomplete thought from the merely lazy thought — though I'm rarely able to do so myself.

~ * ~

The Cheerfulness of a Book. In one of his letters, Nietzsche details how, in October of 1865, he discovered Schopenhauer's book *The World as Will and Representation* in a used bookstore in Leipzig. He writes:

> One day I found this book in a second-hand bookshop, picked it up as something quite unknown to me and turned the pages. I do not know what demon whispered to me "Take this home with you." It was contrary to my usual practice of hesitating over the purchase of books. Once at home, I threw myself onto the sofa with the newly-won treasure and began to let that energetic and gloomy genius operate upon me....

For Nietzsche, the spell was to last for some time. So great is his enthusiasm that he will even attempt to convert others to Schopenhauer's philosophy, often unsuccessfully. Later, Nietzsche regarded pessimism as something to be overcome, a saying "yes" to this world, as it is, unfortunate, indifferent, tragic. Nietzsche often names this horizon a "Dionysian pessimism." But the stakes are high, perhaps too high — even for Nietzsche. There is a sense in which the entirety of Nietzsche's philosophy is a sustained, concerted attempt to shake pessimism.

What I've always wanted to know is who sold back those volumes of Schopenhauer to that used bookstore? One usually sells a book back out of disappointment. Occasionally, one sells a book back out of enthusiasm.

~ * ~

A philosophy exists between the axiom and the sigh. Pessimism is the wavering, the hovering.

~ * ~

A Manual of Style: the bad joke, the "to do" list, the epitaph.

~ * ~

Pessimism is the last refuge of hope.

~ * ~

Dare one hope for a philosophy of futility? Phosphorescent, moss-ridden aphorisms inseparable from the ossification of our own bodies.

~ * ~

The Corpse of a Book. Sometime around 1658, Pascal conceived of an ambitious work of religious philosophy, to be called *Apology for the Christian Religion*. The work was never completed, cut short by Pascal's death four years later. What remains of the work — now known as the *Pensées* — is perhaps one of the most unfinished books in the history of philosophy.

Admittedly, Pascal is partially to blame for the confusion. He wrote his many fragments on large sheets of paper, separating each by a horizontal line. When a sheet was full, he would then cut the paper along the horizontal lines, so that each fragment was self-contained on a strip of paper. These strips of paper where then grouped into piles. Pascal then poked a hole in the top corner of each of the strips, and joined them by running a thread through the hole, forming a bundle. Many of the bundles were thematically grouped — for instance, fragments on human vanity, or boredom, or religious despair were each sewn together. But other bundles don't appear to have any thematic grouping, and many of the fragments are not sewn together at all. What the reader confronts is a book that is, in every way, unbound.

What strikes me is the care Pascal put into his bundles, threading them together like fabric, or a wound. On the evening of the 23rd of November 1654, Pascal had what scholars refer to as his "second conversion." It is recorded in a short text known as "The Memorial." Composed of terse, mystical visions of fire and light, it was written by Pascal on a tiny piece of paper. The paper was sewn into the inside of Pascal's coat, so that it was always near his heart, and it was discovered on him when he died.

I don't know why, but part of me is secretly disappointed that Pascal didn't actually sew "The Memorial" directly into his flesh, perhaps threading it just below his left nipple. There it might fester and flower forth from his chest in lyrical, tendril-like growths of unreflective black opal, gradually submerging his entire body — and later his corpse — into so many distillate specks of ashen thought.

~ * ~

Kierkegaard: life is a tightrope.

Nietzsche: life is a jump rope.

Kafka: life is a trip rope.

Schopenhauer: life is a noose.

Cioran: life is a noose, improperly tied.

~ * ~

The Perfume of a Book. In his last productive year, Nietzsche looked back at this first book, noting how, with pride or relief, "the cadaverous perfume of Schopenhauer stuck to only a few pages."

~ * ~

The Ruins of a Book. Schopenhauer's *The World as Will and Representation* is one of the great failures of systematic philosophy. What begins with the shimmering architectonics of Kant ends up crumbling into dubious arguments, irascible indictments against humanity, nocturnal evocations of the vanity of all being, cryptic quotes from the *Upanishads*, and stark, aphoristic phrases entombed within dense prose, prose that trails off in meditations on nothingness. Schopenhauer, the *depressive* Kantian.

~ * ~

The notion of an American pessimism is an oxymoron, which is as good a reason as any to undertake it.

~ * ~

Impersonal sadness. To become overgrown, like a ruin.

~ * ~

A Master Class in the Aphorism. Nietzsche uses several techniques in his aphorisms. There are, for example, Nietzsche's frequent spells of enthusiasm, which suddenly burst through the layers of irony and sarcasm he has so carefully constructed. For instance, following a weighty critique of morality, we get this: "... forward on the track of wisdom with a firm step and a steady confidence! Whatever you are, serve as your own source of experience! Throw off the dissatisfaction with your nature, pardon yourself for your own self, for in every case you have in yourself a ladder with a hundred rungs...." And so on.

As a student, when I first read such passages, I wanted to jump up with Nietzsche in affirmation. Now, re-reading them, I almost look down in embarrassment. How should one balance the stark, cynical critique of the human condition with such explosions of sincerity? The fault is mine, I'm sure, not Nietzsche's. I have, it seems, become immune to his enthusiasm.

~ * ~

Philosophers are often book lovers, though not all book lovers are alike. The distance that separates the bibliophile from the bibliomaniac is the same distance that separates the optimist from the pessimist.

~ * ~

The Tunnel at the End of the Light. "As the strata of the earth preserve in their order the living creatures of past epochs, so do the shelves of libraries preserve in their order the past errors and their expositions."

Schopenhauer's words are uniquely expressed in a place like Angkor Wat, the temple city whose main entrance houses two massive libraries, now empty. Standing in them today, one feels one is inside a tomb.

~ * ~

From a blurred horizon, quiet black-basalt pools bore into the rocks and our own patiently-withering bones. Slumbering swells of a salt-borne amnesia course through our fibrous limbs. Scorched, wandering brine secretes from every pore.

~ * ~

One always *admits* to being a pessimist.

~ * ~

In tall lichen forests dreams silently hang — anomie of every living cadaver. Towering assemblies of bird, bark, and branching obsidian sway in a tenebrous delirium, asking nothing, accepting everything.

Pessimism's propositions have all the *gravitas* of a bad joke.

~ * ~

We have yet to consider the possibility that depression is purely material, maybe even elemental. Cioran: "Left to its own devices, depression would demolish even the fingernails."

~ * ~

The Sepulcher a Book. Nietzsche once commented that he could never completely follow Schopenhauer's pessimism because, in saying "no" to the world it must eventually negate itself — it is a form of thought that constantly undermines itself. In fact, Schopenhauer was so successful at being this type of pessimist that a reviewer of one of his books assumed that Schopenhauer was already dead (he was not — but found the review disappointing nevertheless).

~ * ~

"Are you a pessimist?"
"On my better days...."

~ * ~

"Nothing is more unbearable to a person than to be in a state of repose, without passion, without occupation, without distractions, without purpose. One then feels one's nothingness, one's abandon, one's insufficiency, one's dependency, one's powerlessness, one's emptiness. Straightaway there arises from the soul *ennui*, depression, sorrow, spite, despair." In passages like these, one senses that Pascal was almost looking forward to it.

~ * ~

Plankton-fed, sleep-drugged eyes cast down in the direction of the sacred.

~ * ~

In distant stellar mornings, lush, verdantique shapes hover noiselessly on the slightest sound. Entire forests levitate.

~ * ~

On Accedie. Partially exhausted. Somewhat tired.

~ * ~

Rosary of stars, seaweed skins, the once-warmed, opaque gems of night. Every thought an ember. Sleep descends, sleep ascends.

~ * ~

The Ether of a Book. Occasionally, one discovers there are books that are written *not* to be read. They are penned by obscure and neglected authors, most of whom have gone mad or mysteriously disappeared. The books themselves are difficult to find; if one is lucky there is a dusty old copy in the Miskatonic University library (though you will most likely find it has mysteriously gone missing). One almost never mentions them casually (e.g., "What are you reading?" "Oh nothing, just the *Necronomicon*"). When they are mentioned, they are mentioned with ominous ceremony. The dreaded *Necronomicon*, the unmentionable *Book of Eibon*, the blasphemous *De Vermis Mysteriis*.

The idea that a person might be driven mad by a book is fantastical, even absurd — especially today, as physical books themselves seem to be vanishing into an ether of oblique and agglomerating metadata. We are so used to consuming books for the information they contain that we rarely consider the possibility that the books might in turn consume us. Thomas Frognall Dibdin's *The Bibliomania; or, Book-Madness* (1809) uses a quasi-medical diagnosis to describe individuals consumed by books, obsessed not just with their contents, but with their materiality: "There is, first, a passion for Large Paper Copies; secondly, for Uncut Copies; thirdly, for Illustrated Copies; fourthly, for Unique Copies; fifthly, for Copies printed upon Vellum; sixthly, for First Editions; seventhly, for True Editions; and eighthly, for Books printed in the Black-Letter."

Holbrook Jackson's *Anatomy of Bibliomania* (1930) goes further, tracing that fine line where the love of books (bibliophilia) turns into book madness (bibliomania). And the madness of possessing books turns with great subtlety into the madness of being possessed by books. Jackson even recounts what is no doubt the pinnacle of bibliomania — the "bibliophages," who are so consumed by their books that they eat them, devoutly incorporating them into their anatomies, effacing all distinction between the literal and the figurative.

Beyond this there is the "bibliosomniac," or the book-sleeper. Briefly mentioned in the *Commentario Philobiblon*, a anonymous commentary on Richard de Bury's mid-14th century treatise, the book-sleeper is defined as "a special type of monk, one who is asleep like a book [*codex*]."

~ * ~

Every person has a point beyond which life is no longer worth living. In this way we are all covert pessimists.

~ * ~

To assemble a lexicon of futility — why the philosopher is really a librarian, the poet a book-thief.

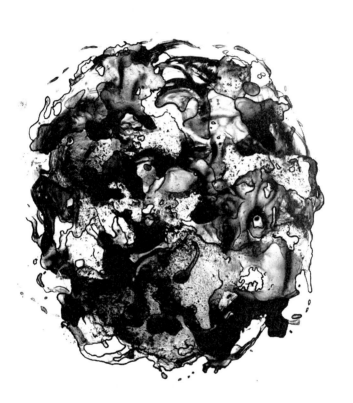

~ * ~

On Bibliomania. It is striking how many of the works of pessimism are incomplete — Pascal's *Pensées*, Leopardi's *Zibaldone*, Lichtenberg's *Sudelbücher*, Joubert's *Carnets*, the stray fragments of Csath, Kafka, Klíma, Pessoa....These are not just works that the author was unable to complete, cut short by illness, depression, or distraction. These are works designed for incompletion — their very existence renders them dubious. I like to think this is why such works were so precious to their authors — but also so insignificant, a drawer of paper scraps, in no particular order, abandoned at one's death, like one's own corpse.

Still, even an incomplete work can be finished.

~ * ~

Arabesque ink wandering winds itself around our ovate dreams. We seem to speak only in the imprecise geometries of black volcanic sands. Huge, impossibly regular shapes of rutted charcoal rocks hover above us, as if waiting.

~ * ~

"I leaf through books, I do not study them"
(Montaigne).

~ * ~

Among the hundreds of pages that comprise the
Anatomy of Melancholy, Burton provides this, his
shortest and most concise definition: "Melancholy
is the character of mortality." He also adds that
melancholy is a chronic condition.

~ * ~

A sigh is the final stage of lyricism.

~ * ~

In his enigmatically-titled book *The Apotheosis of
Groundlessness*, Lev Shestov writes: "When a
person is young he writes because it seems to him
he has discovered a new almighty truth which he
must make haste to impart to forlorn humankind.
Later, becoming more modest, he begins to doubt

his truths: and then he tries to convince himself. A few more years go by, and he knows he was mistaken all round, so there is no need to convince himself. Nevertheless he continues to write, because he is not fit for any other work, and to be accounted a superfluous person is so horrible."

~ * ~

The luminous point where logic becomes contemplation. Lost in thought. Dreamless sleep. Adrift in deep space.

~ * ~

Behind every assertion "is not" lies the admission "not is."

~ * ~

Media vita in morte sumus. Do philosophers also die philosophically? Nietzsche and Schopenhauer provide what are, arguably, the two poles in this debate. Nietzsche's end is filled with great drama, filled with so many scheming characters and plot twists that it is even melodramatic. His now-mythical collapse in Turin, while embracing a flogged horse; the numerous attempts to "cure" him, including one by an art therapist (which failed); the short, effusive, *Wahnbreife* or "madness letters" that are his last writings; the menacing care of his sister, dressing him up in priestly white robes so that fawning followers could make pilgrimage to the "mad philosopher"; the eleven ensuing years of illness, paralysis, and silence, before his death on the 25th of August, 1900. And Nietzsche's death was just the beginning, for his manuscripts were about to be published....

By contrast, Schopenhauer's death was both undramatic and uneventful. He simply passed away in his sleep on the morning of September 21st, 1860. A few months earlier, Schopenhauer had written to a sickly friend with some advice: "Sleep is the source of all health and energy, even of the intellectual sort. I sleep 7, often 8 hours, sometimes 9."

Which death, then, is the more "philosophical"? Perhaps neither. A third option presents itself: that of the 18th century French author Nicolas Chamfort, a writer admired by both Schopenhauer and Nietzsche for his pessimistic aphorisms. On the evening of September 10th of 1793, Chamfort was about to be imprisoned for his criticisms of the French government. Rather than be taken prisoner, he resolved to kill himself. According to a friend, Chamfort calmly finished his dinner, excused himself, and went into his bedroom, where he loaded a pistol and fired it at his forehead. But he missed, injuring his nose and blowing out his right eye. Grabbing a razor, he then tried to slit his own throat — several times. Still alive, he then stabbed himself repeatedly in the heart, but to no avail. His final effort was to cut both wrists, but this again failed to produce the desired effect. Overcome with either pain or frustration, he cried out and collapsed into a chair. Barely alive, he reportedly said, "What can you expect? One never manages to do anything successfully, even killing oneself."

The pessimist, who fails to die....

~ * ~

One never writes a book of fragments. What one ends up with is less than a book. Or more than a book.

~ * ~

A black glow in the deepest sleepwalking seas, invisible like our crystalline joints and our fibrous limbs and as tangible as our tenebrous theaters of doubt.

Univocal Publishing
123 North 3rd Street, #202
Minneapolis, MN 55401
univocalpublishing.com

ISBN 9781937561475

Jason Wagner, Drew S. Burk
(Editors)

This work was composed in
Berkley and Block.

All materials were printed and bound
in June 2015 at Univocal's atelier
in Minneapolis, USA.

The paper is Hammermill 98.
The letterpress cover was printed
on Neenah Classic Crest, Epic Black.
Both are archival quality and acid-free.